SACRED space

Cultivating Your Personal EDEN in a Fallen World

by MERCY HOPE

Sacred Space: Cultivating Your Personal Eden in a Fallen World

Published by 1:11 Publishing
An imprint of Little Dozen Press
Crystal Beach, ON, Canada
littledozen.com

ISBN: 978-1-927658-49-9

one11ministries.com
one11ministries@gmail.com

DEDICATION

To my **Nephews** and **Nieces**

Since the day you were born,
I have prayed that you would walk closely
with your Creator all the days of your life.
You bring so much joy to my heart.
I love you always.

ACKNOWLEDGMENTS

Kim: for being a true kingdom sister
and supporting me through every step
of this writing process.

Drew: for stepping in when this book
was at a standstill and helping me sort out
my jumble of content. You did in two days
what I couldn't do in two years.

Rachel: for being more than a great editor.
You are a true kindred.

Carolyn: ministry alongside you has been a joy.

My heartfelt thanks to each of you.

TABLE OF CONTENTS

AN INVITATION

There is a hidden place inside each one of us. Like a secret walled garden where we are meant to meet with the One who created us. Discovering and cultivating that sacred space is what this book is about.

Enter a tapestry of Scripture woven with deeply personal perspectives and experiences, shared to evoke your spiritual hunger.

Sacred Space is *not* a "how to" manual. Far from it. It is an invitation to something that can never be relegated to words on a page.

Today is the day to begin reclaiming the depth of relationship that is meant to be yours with your Creator.

1

THE MASTER POTTER

Once, after I had already finished sharing my testimony of coming to know God as my Father on a radio interview, the host asked, "So when did you ask Jesus into your heart?"

Um, *awkward.*

See, out of fear of going to hell, I technically "asked Jesus into my heart" via the sinner's prayer as a young girl many times. But that really had nothing to do with my ultimate salvation.

You want even more awkward? I was filled with the Holy Spirit, spoke in tongues, and had God speak to me and tell me He would be a Father to me all before I actually understood the point of the cross or even who Jesus was.

It was complicated. And that was just the first day of my journey with God. It stayed complicated.

After all that, I went through a seven-year period where I was so disappointed and angry with God that I thought He had taken His Spirit from me. Seriously, my teen years were lousy when it came to my inner life!

I had no perspective of the things I've written about in this book. The concept of "sacred space" wasn't real to me yet. I couldn't feel God or even find the words to talk to Him. I once again felt estranged from my Father. But after what felt like an eternity, once I was ready to stop blaming Him for the hard things in my life and became aware that I desperately wanted Him again, He breathed into me a second time. It was like spiritual CPR. Twenty years later, He remains the breath in my lungs, and I refuse to let anything separate us.

In my mind, I have a version of how redemption should take place. If I was writing a thesis on the process of salvation, it might look something like:

1. Understand the fall and redemption.

2. Repent and believe.

3. Be water baptized/publicly confess faith.

4. Receive Holy Spirit baptism.

5. Consistently grow in relationship with Jesus.

Oh, and all that within the context of a healthy faith-family.

The problem is my own journey has been

> MY OWN JOURNEY
> HAS BEEN WAY MESSIER
> THAN THE THEOLOGY
> I COULD PUT ON PAPER.

way messier than the theology I could put on paper.

My testimony is best summarized by the Scripture that says, "He lifted me out of the pit of despair, out of the mud and the mire. He set my feet on solid ground and steadied me as I walked along" (Psalm 40:2, NLT).

In a sense, before God lifted me out, I was PART of that mud—totally enmeshed in the experiences of my past. I couldn't give my own life shape or meaning. I was clay needing to be formed. Actually, that part hasn't changed. I'm still clay, just the kind the Creator can work with. My life has been messy the way pottery is messy. But it's turning out (pardon the pun) pretty well.

One of my favorite things in the world is to sit down at a pottery wheel and create. The clay is soft and pliable in my hands. *Spinning.* I apply pressure. *Clay spinning under my fingers and palms.* If it gets a little dry, I reach for the wet sponge and add water. *Still spinning.* Thumbs join the dance of giving shape to the lump. *Still spinning.* Then the pulling begins. *Still spinning.* If the pot starts to wobble, I hold my hands steady until the piece becomes centered again. *Still spinning.*

Then, the spinning stops. I think it is perfect. I can't wait to paint. It is my masterpiece.

I am not a master potter. I am an amateur. But still, to me, my creation is lovely. Our Creator, on the other hand, *is* a Master Potter.

Each of us was handcrafted by the fingers of God in our mother's womb. It is incredible to contemplate that He sticks His fingers in the "clay" of our DNA, fashions a masterpiece, and then adds the breath of life to our lungs.

There is so much about all this that I don't understand. Because God is working with the materials of a fallen world, there are questions I can't answer—like why people are born with birth defects, or why some children never get to take their first breath. What I

> EVERY PERSON IS
> A MASTERPIECE FROM
> THE GIVER OF LIFE.

do know is that every person is a masterpiece made by the Giver of Life.

As Jesus said, "A thief comes only to steal and to kill and to destroy. I have come that they may have life and have it in abundance" (John 10:10).

I love how God created the first man from the dust in Genesis, and then later in Scripture He uses the imagery of a potter and clay.

Our Creator says in the book of Isaiah:

You have turned things around, as if the potter were the same as the clay. How can what is made say about its maker, "He didn't make me"? How can what is formed say about the one who formed it, "He doesn't understand what he's doing"?

Woe to the one who argues with his Maker—one clay pot among many. Does clay say to the one forming it: What are you making? Or does your work say: He has no hands? How absurd is the one who says to his father: "What are you fathering?" or to his mother: "What are you giving birth to?"

This is what the LORD, the Holy One of Israel and its Maker, says: "Ask Me what is to happen to My sons, and instruct Me about the work of My hands.

I made the earth, and created man on it. It was My hands that stretched out the heavens, and I commanded all their host." (Isaiah 29:16, 45:9–12)

This is the word that came to Jeremiah from the LORD: "Go down at once to the potter's house; there I will reveal My words to you." So I went down to the potter's house, and there he was, working away at the wheel. But the jar that he was making from the clay became flawed in the potter's hand, so he made it into another jar, as it seemed right for him to do. The word of the LORD came to me: "House of Israel, can I not treat you as this potter treats his clay?"—this is the LORD's declaration. "Just like clay in the potter's hand, so are you in My hand, house of Israel." (Jeremiah 18:1–6)

The potter and clay analogy is even referenced in the New Testament:

> But who are you, a human being, to talk back to God? "Shall what is formed say to the one who formed it, 'Why did you make me like this?'" Does not the potter have the right to make out of the same lump of clay some pottery for special purposes and some for common use? (Romans 9:20, NIV)

My Creator has remade me many times over. I get stuck in a warp, get a chip on my shoulder, get bent out of shape. He continues to work on me, molding me back into usable shape.

I've experienced moments where I felt like a glamorous display piece among the famous and powerful, wondering, *How in the world did I make it here?* Other seasons I've felt like a bedpan. But He's there through it all, faithfully shaping and remaking me in needed ways.

Over time I've discovered the beauty in this process. For me, redemption has been far more than a one-time prayer. It is a never-ending, hands-on relationship. Even when I thought God's Spirit had left me, He hadn't. Even when I couldn't feel Him, His hands were still keeping me from flying apart.

> EVEN WHEN I COULDN'T FEEL HIM, HIS HANDS WERE STILL KEEPING ME FROM FLYING APART.

Now I say with gratitude, "Yet LORD, You are our Father; we are the clay, and You are our potter; we all are the work of Your hands" (Isaiah 64:8).

Even more than I love spinning pottery, I love being held under the hands of the Potter.

2

WHO IS JESUS TO YOU?

Thirteen years ago, I was at a conference where Judy Jacobs was ministering. I have a special place in my heart for that woman of God! Through a prophetic word and personal prayer, she imparted something to me that day that changed my life and ministry forever. But while Judy was still on stage, the Holy Spirit said to me, "Many people want to come and be around her anointing, but very few will pay the price for the anointing themselves."

It's true. Looking around me, I could see that many people wanted to be near Judy—and it's not just her. When someone has a close and powerful walk with God, others are drawn to them. In some cases, large crowds will gather. They may want to see a miracle, or hear a prophetic word, or simply experience the presence of God. They want to be around the anointing. But few seem to personally seek out this depth of relationship with Jesus.

What is truly astounding about this whole thing is that the price of having God's presence in our lives is primarily surrender to His love and will. The price is our willingness to be available to our Creator. To sit at His feet with a heart attitude of worship and focused love (Luke 10:39).

I don't want to chase His presence as it rests on someone else. I want to be a resting place for His presence.

Jesus has never sought out fans. He wants friends who know Him personally. You know, the kind of friends who are actually family. Look at this incredible interaction Jesus had with His disciples:

> I WANT TO BE A RESTING PLACE FOR HIS PRESENCE.

> When Jesus came to the region of Caesarea Philippi, He asked His disciples, "Who do people say that the Son of Man is?" And they said, "Some say John the Baptist; others, Elijah; still others, Jeremiah or one of the prophets."
>
> "But you," He asked them, "who do you say that I am?" Simon Peter answered, "You are the Messiah, the Son of the living God!"
>
> And Jesus responded, "Simon son of Jonah, you are blessed because flesh

and blood did not reveal this to you, but My Father in heaven . . . And I also say to you that you are Peter, and on this rock I will build My church, and the forces of Hades will not overpower it. I will give you the keys of the kingdom of heaven, and whatever you bind on earth is already bound in heaven, and whatever you loose on earth is already loosed in heaven." (Matthew 16:13–19)

On the rock of revelation that Yeshua was the Messiah (or to use the more familiar Greek-based wording, that Jesus was the Christ), the church was built.[1]

Because of who Jesus is, and because of Peter's personal knowledge of it, the kingdom of heaven would be released, and the kingdom of darkness would not win. But if Peter had pref-

---

[1] If you think Jesus was saying the church was built on Peter himself, that's cool too. This is just my rendering.

aced his final statement of "You are the Christ" with "Some say," I am sure it would not have elicited the same response from Jesus.

Jesus wasn't asking what Peter and the others had heard about Him from other people. He wanted to know who *they knew* Him to be.

When I start thinking about who Jesus is to me, words immediately start flowing out of my heart. He is my:

Light who guides my way.

Rock when everything around me is shaking.

Shield when the enemy's arrows are flying my way.

Defender when I'm accused.

Faithful One.

Anchor when the stormy winds are harsh.

Healer when I'm wounded.

Savior.

Rescuer.

Redeemer.

Jesus is kinder than we think.

He is more patient than we have ever dreamed.

He is more powerful than our imaginations can portray.

He is holier than we can fathom.

He loves at a depth that we have barely even begun to delve into.

Our mortal minds cannot grasp His essence.

We all need our minds renewed and expanded when it comes to seeing Jesus for who He truly is.

But at the end of the day, my happiest

thought is that He truly knows me more than any human ever could. "I am my Beloved's, and He is mine" (Song of Solomon 6:3).

In 1834, Edward Mote penned one of my favorite hymns, saying who he knew Jesus to be. His declaration was this:

> My hope is built on nothing less
> Than Jesus' blood and righteousness;
> I dare not trust the sweetest frame,
> But wholly lean on Jesus' name.
>
> When darkness veils His lovely face,
> I rest on His unchanging grace;
> In every high and stormy gale,
> My anchor holds within the veil.
>
> His oath, His covenant, His blood
> Support me in the whelming flood;
> When all around my soul gives way,
> He then is all my hope and stay.

When He shall come with trumpet sound,

Oh, may I then in Him be found;

Dressed in His righteousness alone,

Faultless to stand before the throne.

On Christ, the solid Rock, I stand;

All other ground is sinking sand,

All other ground is sinking sand.

To know my Creator and walk as closely to Him as is humanly possible is my ultimate pursuit. When I was younger, that pursuit often felt like a *Fast and Furious* car race. As I get older it feels more like continuing to put one foot in front of the other, refusing to give up even when I'm weary and the path is covered in dense fog. Pushing through the fatigue, pain, discouragement, warfare, wounds, exhaustion, and questions to clear a path and cultivate a garden for Him to establish Himself within me.

I regularly tell those I mentor that life is

hard. So you can do hard life walking hand in hand with your Creator, or you can do hard life on your own, trying to figure it out yourself. I personally choose to walk with my Creator all the days of my life and beyond. He is everything to me. He is my safe place in a world that is sometimes terrifying.

> HE IS MY
> SAFE PLACE
> IN A WORLD THAT
> IS SOMETIMES
> TERRIFYING.

How about you? If Jesus were standing in front of you right now, looking into your eyes, and He asked you, "Who do you say I am?" What would you say?

I encourage you to make this question personal and applicable. Write down what flows out of your heart as you meet with Him in your sacred space. Who do you know Him to be?

3
SACRED SPACE:
A PERSONAL EDEN

I used to wonder how people could sing worship songs that said things like, "I will have no other lover." I would think, *How can you say that as a married person? How can you say you have no other loves when you clearly love your kids so much?* But later I came to differentiate.

There is a place in the soul—a sacred space—a proverbial garden—where only He can enter and be worshiped. In that place, there is no competition. No one else can access the space that is meant for an interactive relationship with our Creator. If it is not filled by His Holy Spirit, it simply remains vacant.

You may be asking where I see a biblical basis for a personal Eden or why I use the analogy of a garden.

In Genesis, Eden was the original garden of God, the place of meeting between Creator and creation.

Song of Songs refers to the bride—historically regarded as an analogy of God's people, with the Bridegroom being analogous to Christ—as a "locked garden." This imagery highlights to me that this is no public park and certainly not a thoroughfare.

Isaiah and Jeremiah later refer to the people of the LORD as a "well-watered garden."

> The LORD will always lead you, satisfy
> you in a parched land, and strengthen

your bones. You will be like a watered garden and like a spring whose waters never run dry. (Isaiah 58:11)

They will come and shout for joy on the heights of Zion; they will be radiant with joy because of the LORD's goodness, because of the grain, the new wine, the fresh oil, and because of the young of the flocks and herds. Their life will be like an irrigated garden, and they will no longer grow weak from hunger. (Jeremiah 31:12)

Conversely, Isaiah warns the rebels of Israel, "For you will become . . . like a garden without water" (Isaiah 1:30).

In Luke 8:5–8, Jesus told the parable of the sower:

A sower went out to sow his seed. As he was sowing, some fell along the path; it was trampled on, and the birds of the sky ate it up. Other seed fell on the rock; when it sprang up, it withered, since it lacked moisture. Other seed fell among thorns; the thorns sprang up with it and choked it. Still other seed fell on good ground; when it sprang up, it produced a crop: 100 times what was sown.

He also gave the interpretation.

This is the meaning of the parable: The seed is the word of God. The seeds along the path are those who have heard. Then the Devil comes and takes away the word from their hearts, so that they may not believe and be saved. And the seeds on the rock are those who, when they hear, welcome the word with joy. Having no root, these believe for a while and depart in a time of testing. As for the seed that fell among thorns, these are the ones who, when they have heard, go on their way and are choked with worries, riches, and pleasures of life, and produce no mature fruit. But the seed in the good ground—these are the ones who, having heard the word with an honest and good heart, hold on to it and by enduring, bear fruit. (Luke 8:11–15)

I want my heart to be good soil. I want God's words to take root and produce good fruit in my life.

Weeds of jealousy, doubt, fear, insecurity, and self-righteousness still spring up more times than I care to admit. But they have no place in my enclosed garden. When I am sitting with Him in this sacred space, those things look completely out of place. They do not cultivate an atmosphere of peace. Frankly, they are embarrassing.

At this point in my walk with Him, He doesn't even have to point out the things He doesn't enjoy in my life. His presence just illuminates anything that needs to go. He is always willing to help me prune and do the heavy lifting when I'm ready to surrender.

As Jesus said to His disciples:

> I am the true vine, and My Father is the vineyard keeper. Every branch in Me that does not produce fruit He removes, and He prunes every branch that produces fruit so that it will produce more fruit . . . Remain in Me, and I in you. Just as a branch is unable to produce fruit by itself unless it remains on the vine, so neither can you unless you remain in Me. I am the vine; you are the branches. The one who remains in Me and I in him produces much fruit, because you can do noth-

ing without Me. If anyone does not remain in Me, he is thrown aside like a branch and he withers. They gather them, throw them into the fire, and they are burned. If you remain in Me and My words remain in you, ask whatever you want and it will be done for you. My Father is glorified by this: that you produce much fruit and prove to be My disciples. (John 15:1–2, 4–8)

See the relationship and the interconnectedness? I am in Him. He is in me. I am His. He is mine. He created a planet for me to live on and a body for me to live in. I surrender my body and soul back to Him and cultivate a garden for Him to live inside of me.

This is the relational aspect of the garden. In the garden of my soul, we walk together, talk together, prune together. He does most of the watering, and I nurture what He plants in the soil of me. Then, together we sit back and enjoy the fruit of our labors. I am awestruck that the Creator of the Universe wants me to co-create something with Him.

THE BIBLE'S GARDEN IMAGERY IS VIVID AND APROPOS.

For me, the Bible's garden imagery is vivid and apropos. It gives me a visual way to assess the state of my inner life with God. You can also think of it as an inner sanctuary, but to me, that feels too sterile. A building takes less maintenance. But a garden requires constant upkeep, attention, and care.

When I picture my inner "garden," I see vines growing up over the walls. Trees both large and small. Lush grass, some spindly weeds, deep green ground cover. Flowering plants of all kinds. A bench. Things that need to be pulled and pruned. But mostly, I see a place of entering rest with my beloved Jesus.

Each of us has a garden that is unique to us. After hearing me preach on this topic, one man asked the Lord to show him his garden, and he saw a vast field. Nothing enclosed. Very minimalist. I don't claim to know what that meant, but it revealed something personal to him.

I encourage you to ask our Creator to show you your garden. What does your inner life look like to Him? What kind of dwelling place have you given Him to occupy? If this is a new concept to you, don't be shocked or discouraged if you find your garden in total disarray. Cultivating your inner life takes time. But the good news is, although this is a partnership, God is the husbandman over the garden. Primarily, we just need to let Him have His way.

There is no fear in this perfect love. I promise you, He is the kindest gardener you will ever meet.

4

THE GOSPEL OF RECONCILIATION

The God written of in the Bible is known to us today as Yahweh, the LORD, the Great I Am, Jehovah, the Word, Jesus, Yeshua, and more. There are so many names and titles for our indescribable God. So you may wonder why in this book, I am choosing to put such a strong emphasis on the Creator aspect of who God is.

I do it for very personal reasons. By going back to the Genesis account of creation and relating to God as my Creator, I've gained a much greater understanding of why Jesus came to earth, and it has deepened my relationship with Him. Truly, knowing God as my Creator has been priceless to me.

On this journey back to Eden, I have realized that having a Creator gives us both identity and accountability. It gives us identity because we know who is the reason for our existence. We really do have a Father in heaven. Reconciliation to our Creator means we are no longer orphans. Not only that, but having a Creator gives us accountability. If we are lost, there is someone who will come looking for us. As the Creator called for Adam in Genesis 3:9, He also seeks us out today.

> HAVING A CREATOR GIVES US BOTH IDENTITY AND ACCOUNTABILITY.

Jesus told His followers, "I will not leave you as orphans; I am coming to you" (John 14:18). He said, "For the Son of Man has come to seek and to save the lost" (Luke 19:10). Matthew tells us, "He came to give his life as the price for setting many people free" (Matthew 20:28, NIrV).

John 1 explains the mystery of Jesus as Creator. The One who spoke the universe into existence became a man:

> In the beginning was the Word, and the Word was with God, and the Word was God. All things were created through Him, and apart from Him not one thing was created that has been created. Life was in Him, and that life was the light of men. That light shines in the darkness, yet the darkness did not overcome it. He was in the world, and the world was created through Him, yet the world did not recognize Him. He

came to His own, and His own people did not receive Him. But to all who did receive Him, He gave them the right to be children of God, to those who believe in His name, who were born, not of blood, or of the will of the flesh, or of the will of man, but of God. The Word became flesh and took up residence among us. We observed His glory, the glory as the One and Only Son from the Father, full of grace and truth. (John 1:1, 3–5, 10–14)

Our Creator came and walked with His creation once again.

Jesus lived out this human existence starting in the womb. His mom, Mary, was a virgin impregnated by the Holy Spirit. His earth dad was a carpenter named Joseph. Jesus walked through the ordinary things of life and endured an agony that is beyond our comprehension.

He experienced life, death, and resurrection.

Because Adam and Eve chose to experientially know good and evil, Jesus became the second Adam to also experience good and evil—*all of it.*

> Because God's children are human beings—made of flesh and blood—the Son also became flesh and blood. For only as a human being could he die, and only by dying could he break the power of the devil, who had the power of death. Only in this way could he set free all who have lived their lives as slaves to the fear of dying . . . Therefore, it was necessary for him to be made in every respect like us, his brothers and sisters, so that he could be our merciful and faithful High Priest before God. Then he could offer a sacrifice that would take away the sins of

the people. Since he himself has gone through suffering and testing, he is able to help us when we are being tested. (Hebrews 2:14–15, 17–18, NLT)

The fact that Jesus came to earth to suffer everything we would ever experience means we are never without the listening ear of someone who truly understands what we are going through. Because Jesus sweat drops of blood alone in a garden (Luke 22:39–44), we can be confident that when we are going through the darkest days of our lives, if we ask, He will meet

> JESUS HAS NEVER FORGOTTEN WHAT IT FEELS LIKE TO BE A BROKEN, BRUISED, EXHAUSTED, DYING HUMAN.

with us in our garden to identify with our suffering. He has never forgotten what it feels like to be a broken, bruised, exhausted, dying human with friends who couldn't even stay awake for Him. His friends weren't there for Him at His darkest hour, but He is faithfully there for us when we need, or want, Him. He is mind-blowingly good like that.

> Nothing in all creation is hidden from God. Everything is naked and exposed before his eyes, and he is the one to whom we are accountable. So then, since we have a great High Priest who has entered heaven, Jesus the Son of God, let us hold firmly to what we believe. This High Priest of ours understands our weaknesses, for he faced all of the same testings we do, yet he did not sin. So let us come boldly to the throne of our gracious God. There we will receive his mercy, and we will find grace to help us when we need it most. (Hebrews 4:13–16)

In the Old Testament, we see a few people who walked in close relationship with their Creator. Examples include Enoch, Moses, and David. But when Jesus came, He tore the veil and invited anyone who wanted to walk in close relationship with Him to come.

In one of his letters to the Corinthians, the apostle Paul clearly lays out what the "good news" is: *We can be reconciled to God.* We can have the relationship with our Creator that He has always desired to have with us.

> The first man was from the earth and made of dust; the second man is from heaven. And just as we have borne the image of the man made of dust, we will also bear the image of the heavenly man. (1 Corinthians 15:47)

> This means that anyone who belongs to Christ has become a new person. The old life is gone; a new life has begun!

And all of this is a gift from God, who brought us back to himself through Christ. And God has given us this task of reconciling people to him. For God was in Christ, reconciling the world to himself, no longer counting people's sins against them. And he gave us this wonderful message of reconciliation. So we are Christ's ambassadors; God is making his appeal through us. We speak for Christ when we plead, "Come back to God!" For God made Christ, who never sinned, to be the offering for our sin, so that we could be made right with God through Christ. (2 Corinthians 5:17–21, NLT)

RECONCILIATION MEANS THAT WE CAN NOW HAVE AN UNHINDERED RELATIONSHIP WITH OUR CREATOR AND REDEEMER.

Reconciliation means that we can now have an unhindered relationship with the One who is both Creator and Redeemer.

> He has enabled you to share in the inheritance that belongs to his people, who live in the light. For he has rescued us from the kingdom of darkness and transferred us into the Kingdom of his dear Son, who purchased our freedom and forgave our sins. Christ is the visible image of the invisible God. He existed before anything was created and is supreme over all creation, for through him God created everything in the heavenly realms and on earth. He made the things we can see and the things we can't see—such as thrones, kingdoms, rulers, and authorities in the unseen world. Everything was created through him and for him. He existed before anything else, and he holds

all creation together. Christ is also the head of the church, which is his body. He is the beginning, supreme over all who rise from the dead. So he is first in everything. For God in all his fullness was pleased to live in Christ, and through him God reconciled everything to himself. He made peace with everything in heaven and on earth by means of Christ's blood on the cross. This includes you who were once far away from God. You were his enemies, separated from him by your evil thoughts and actions. Yet now he has reconciled you to himself through the death of Christ in his physical body. (Colossians 1:12b-22a, NLT)

Our Creator came for us. There should be nothing left for Him to prove. Now He wants us to come to Him.

5

LEGITIMATE ACCESS
TO THE GARDEN

Have you ever wished you had a rich uncle to help fund a life dream? I'll admit I have.

Or maybe you are one of the envied few who knows the reality of such a thing. I have a friend who is the privileged niece of a wealthy uncle. He enjoys being generous toward her. Because of my relationship with her, I could potentially access some of the benefits of the relationship she has with him. For instance, if I was traveling with her I could stay at her uncle's upscale condo, swim in his infinity pool, and go out on his yacht. Maybe even drop his name to gain access to the clubhouse. All that without ever meeting him myself. To me, he is some guy out there whose relationship to my friend creates a perk for me.

But if I have a personal need, I have no access to him. I don't have his cell phone number, and even if his niece gave it to me, he would not recognize my voice if I called him. He is not going to fund my next ministry trip to the Philippines. *He doesn't know me.*

The disconcerting reality is that this is how I see many people living out Christianity, especially in North America: treating Jesus like their friend's rich uncle. Many see no need to know Him for themselves. They just want to know enough about Him to get into the proverbial clubhouse.

Crowds stream into churches, home groups,

and ministries, often brought by a friend. People can quickly learn the lingo. Depending on the denominational context, they learn to raise their hands and dance, or sit reverently still and then stand to recite the liturgy. Pretty soon, they are "in." They may even be assigned leadership positions. My question is, how many people are legitimately coming *into Christ* versus merely coming into Christian circles? I'm concerned that many, many people are in the church, but they are not *in Christ.*

In John 10:1–16, Jesus foretold that people would "climb over the wall" instead of going through the Door.

> "I assure you: Anyone who doesn't enter the sheep pen by the door but climbs in some other way, is a thief and a robber. The one who enters by the door is the shepherd of the sheep. The doorkeeper opens it for him, and

the sheep hear his voice. He calls his own sheep by name and leads them out. When he has brought all his own outside, he goes ahead of them. The sheep follow him because they recognize his voice. They will never follow a stranger; instead they will run away from him, because they don't recognize the voice of strangers."

Jesus gave them this illustration, but they did not understand what He was telling them. So Jesus said again, "I assure you: I am the door of the sheep. All who came before Me are thieves and robbers, but the sheep didn't listen to them. I am the door. If anyone enters by Me, he will be saved and will come in and go out and find pasture. A thief comes only to steal and to kill and to destroy. I have come that they may have life and have it in abundance. I am the good shepherd. The good shepherd lays down his life for the sheep. The hired man, since he is not the shepherd and doesn't own the sheep, leaves them and runs away when he sees a wolf coming. The wolf then snatches and scatters them. This happens because he is a hired man and doesn't care about the sheep. I am the good shepherd. I know My own sheep, and they know Me, as the Father knows Me, and I know the Father."

Jesus's sheepfold illustration points to the fact that in some instances, "climbing in some other way" is a sinister act. But it seems to me that there also exists an element of people who are simply not being shown the Door, and so they jump over the wall out of lack of understanding or direction.

As an evangelist, I want to make the message crystal clear that Jesus is the Door. When lost sons and daughters find their way to Him, He liberates them from the slavery of sin and gifts them with immortality. Jesus Christ gives us our place of belonging in His family. There is no other way. No other Name. No one else was worthy of spilling His blood for our redemption.

Recently, my friend Kim (who is a true kingdom sister) and I were prepping to share on this topic of garden intimacy. The particular audience is accustomed to regularly sitting under anointed ministers. So, no pressure, right?

Like our audience, Kim and I have heard hundreds of powerful sermons. We didn't want to just recycle a worn-out message. We wanted to bring a "fresh bread" kind of message that night that would take us all deeper into the heart of our Creator.

As we sat on her couch praying for the upcoming event, a scene played out in front of me. I saw the entrance to the original garden of Eden. I saw the cherub posted there to guard it and the flaming, spinning sword blocking the way so that fallen humanity could not regain entrance and eat from the tree of life (see Genesis 3:24).

But what I saw next was incredible! Jesus appeared, approached the cherub, and said, "You are relieved of your duty. I'll take it from here." The cherub bowed his head and stepped aside as a soldier would submit to his commanding officer. Then Jesus Himself stood in the entrance, stretched His arms out (and by doing so became the Door), and said with a loud voice, "Whoever will, let them come!"

I was overwhelmed, and I could hardly wait to share what I had just seen! Getting to tell the ancient truths of God's Word, along with this fresh vision that had just made them even more real to me, was transformational. I came away from that evening loving my Redeemer even more.

Jesus's arms are open. We have access to enter in and walk and talk with Him as Adam and Eve once did. They chose to eat from the tree of the knowledge of good and evil, but we can choose the tree of life. Eternal life is a restored relationship with our Eternal Father. We do not enter eternal life through knowing a lot about God, but through relationally knowing Him.

Jesus Himself said, "You study the Scriptures diligently because you think that in them you have eternal life. These are the very Scriptures that testify about me, yet you refuse to come to me to have life" (John 5:39–40, NIV). He went on to say, "The one who comes to Me I will never cast out" (John 6:37b).

Jesus is not a means to the end of eternal life, but the end in and of Himself. Jesus is the Creator and sustainer of life, and knowing Him is life eternal.

Our garden of intimacy is restored and established forever when we come into Him and He comes into us (see John 17).

Many people leave Christianity because they only "climbed over the wall" in the first place. They simply joined the club, so when the club disillusions them, they leave. They often lose their faith as well, because it was based on someone else's faith—and that person has now wounded them. It is a heartbreaking pattern. I have seen more individuals than I care to admit leave the faith because their faith was misplaced. This was a motivator for me in writing this book—to say to anyone who is not walking in a restored relationship with their Creator, *you can be reconciled to your Father.*

There is a seat at the Father's table with your name on it, just waiting for you to take your place. He wants you with Him right now and into eternity. It is not too late to take that vulnerable and intimate step of making your relationship with Jesus personal. Not coming in on anyone's coattail. You. Alone in the presence of the One who created you.

For those who are already walking intimately with your Creator, I want to remind you that you can always come closer and go deeper. Plus, you can participate in pointing people to the Door (I mean that in a good way).

I don't just want to be in the clubhouse, or the church, because I name-drop a rich uncle or Jesus. I want legitimate access to Jesus, which is gained by coming through Him. I don't just want to sing "I am a friend of God"—I want the reality of my life to be that I am known in heaven as a friend of God. I know what is on His heart because I am in His heart.

He knows my name. I am His, and He is mine.

6

AN ANCIENT ROMANCE

Married couples will attest that while a good marriage must be maintained in the normal (and even mundane) events of day-to-day life, the intimacy and joy of that relationship are greatly enhanced by date nights and times away from the grind.

What does this have to do with knowing God, you may ask? Well, buckle up your seat belts. We are about to jettison our modern mindsets and replace them with something much deeper as we blast back in time to about 900 BC to a setting of poetry and romance. Are you ready for the journey? We're going back to a text called Song of Songs, which is also known as Song of Solomon.

Song of Songs could be called the erotica of the Bible. But as a single woman who is still a virgin (no, I am not ashamed to admit it), the experiential lens through which I read this text is one of my own intimacy with Christ and His longing for me.

I recognize that some people do not see a relationship with Jesus through this lens. So if you are convinced that Song of Songs is only about King Solomon and a Shulamite woman, and that it does not also prophetically depict Christ (the other "son of David") and the church (the bride of Christ), then you are free to disregard this chapter. I simply could not think of another text that so beautifully reflects the passionate heart of King Jesus toward His bride and our response to Him.

So the son of David says,

> My dove . . . let me see your face, let me hear your voice; for your voice is sweet, and your face is lovely. (Song of Songs 2:14)

> How beautiful you are and how pleasant, my love, with such delights! Your mouth is like fine wine—flowing smoothly for my love, gliding past my lips and teeth! (Song of Songs 7:8–9)

> You are altogether beautiful, my darling, beautiful in every way. You have captured my heart, my treasure, my bride. You hold it hostage with one glance of your eyes, with a single jewel of your necklace. Your love delights me, my treasure, my bride. Your love

is better than wine, your perfume more fragrant than spices. Your lips are as sweet as nectar, my bride. Honey and milk are under your tongue. Your clothes are scented like the cedars of Lebanon. You are my private garden, my treasure, my bride, a secluded spring, a hidden fountain. (Song of Songs 4:7, 9–12, NLT)

Your branches are a paradise of pomegranates with choicest fruits, henna with nard—nard and saffron, calamus and cinnamon, with all the trees of frankincense, myrrh and aloes, with all the best spices. You are a garden spring. (Song of Songs 4:13–15)

I have entered my garden, my treasure, my bride! (Song of Songs 5:1, NLT)

And the bride's response is this:

My love . . . look, he is standing behind our wall, gazing through the windows, peering through the lattice. My love calls to me: Arise, my darling. Come away, my beautiful one. (Song of Songs 2:9–10)

His mouth is sweetness. He is absolutely desirable. This is my love, and this is my friend. (Song of Songs 5:16)

Oh, that he would kiss me with the kisses of his mouth! For your love is more delightful than wine. The fragrance of your perfume is intoxicating; your name is perfume poured out. No wonder young women adore you. Take me with you—let us hurry. Oh, that the king would bring me to his chambers. We will rejoice and be glad for you; we will praise your love more than wine. It is only right that they adore you. While the king is on his couch, my perfume releases its fragrance. (Song of Songs 1:2–4, 12)

I delight to sit in his shade, and his fruit is sweet to my taste. He brought me to the banquet hall, and he looked on me with love. Sustain me . . . for I am love-sick. His left hand is under my head, and his right hand embraces me. (Song of Songs 2:3–6)

Set me as a seal on your heart, as a seal on your arm. For love is as strong as death; ardent love is as unrelenting as Sheol. Love's flames are fiery flames—the fiercest of all. Mighty waters cannot extinguish love; rivers cannot sweep it away. If a man were to give all his wealth for love, it would be utterly scorned. (Song of Songs 7:6–7)

Awaken, north wind—come, south

wind. Blow on my garden, and spread the fragrance of its spices. Let my love come to his garden and eat its choicest fruits. (Song of Songs 4:16)

I belong to my love, and his desire is for me. Come, my love, let's go to the field; let's spend the night among the henna blossoms. Let's go early to the vineyards . . . There I will give you my love. (Song of Songs 6:10–12)

My love is mine and I am his. (Song of Songs 2:16)

The most intimate and passionate expressions of human love in marriage are meant to reflect, albeit dimly, the love of Christ and His bride.

When I read these Scriptures, I can picture our Creator just basking in His bride's unrestrained adoration and worship.

Not everyone sees the point of this poetry, this unabashed gushy love. In John 12 we see that Judas Iscariot was ticked off when Mary poured her expensive anointing oil on Jesus's feet and wiped them with her hair. It must have made Judas super confused and uncomfortable. So he called it a waste. Judas's response was basically, "Why couldn't she just make a donation to our ministry? This behavior is totally unorthodox and uncalled for." But Mary saw what Judas couldn't and experienced what Judas hadn't. Her extravagant act touched and ministered to Jesus, and He called it appropriate. He wasn't embarrassed to receive Mary's outpouring of uncontainable, even unconventional, love.

My guess is that it's largely thanks to the Industrial Revolution that our culture now thinks primarily in terms of productivity. If we are not careful, we can interchange the biblical concept of fruitfulness with our cultural drive for the bottom line. But they are not the same, and they are achieved very differently.

Our Creator did not make us steel parts of

> OUR CREATOR IS
> NOT A MANUFACTURER;
> HE IS AN ARTIST
> AND A HUSBAND.

a machine. He made us living parts of His bride. He is not a manufacturer; He is an Artist and a Husband. He longs for us to be with Him in our sacred space. Not striving. Just being fully present and abandoned to Him, with everything else flowing out of that space.

To Him, this is not a waste.

7

INTIMACY EQUALS ACCESS

The disciple John knew what it meant to be close to Jesus. I love the fact that John has no problem referring to himself as "the disciple whom Jesus loved." He knew he was loved and seemed confident because of it. The other disciples appeared to know it too.

In the account of the Last Supper in John 13, we see John leaning back on Jesus's chest and Peter wanting John to ask Jesus the hard question they were all wondering. Why did the other disciples appoint John instead of asking themselves? Peter never seemed to have a problem before when it came to speaking up.

> INTIMACY EQUALS ACCESS.

But in this sacred moment, I think they all knew that intimacy equals access.

John was the closest one to Jesus. This was definitely true in proximity, but it was true relationally as well. His position gave him the access to ask Jesus the pressing question at hand. See, not only was Jesus a friend to John, but John was a friend to Jesus.[2]

Sometimes, I picture myself like John, leaning back on Jesus's chest. I ask Him to let me hear His heartbeat . . . until my own heart catches the rhythm. This may seem like a

---

2   John 15:15 speaks of friendship with Jesus: "I do not call you slaves anymore, because a slave doesn't know what his master is doing. I have called you friends, because I have made known to you everything I have heard from My Father."

strange way to approach prayer, but I have found that Jesus responds to it—and my life is richer as a result.

As we explore this concept of intimacy with God, I want to look at the word "know" that Jesus uses so many times. For instance, in John 10:14 He says, "I know My own sheep, and they know Me." That word "know" in Greek is *ginosko*. By virtue of being a verb, it is first of all "an action or state of being."

The definition is:

1. to learn to know, come to know, get a knowledge of, perceive, feel
    a. to become known

2. to know, understand, perceive, have knowledge of

3. Jewish idiom for sexual intercourse between a man and a woman

4. to become acquainted with, to know[3]

In other words, it is the word used when speaking of intimacy.

If Jesus were referring to intellectual knowledge, the Greek word used would have been *gnosis*.

Its definition is:

1. knowledge signifies in general intelligence, understanding

   a. the general knowledge of Christian religion

   b. the deeper more perfect and enlarged knowledge of this religion, such as belongs to the more advanced

   c. esp. of things lawful and unlawful for Christians

   d. moral wisdom, such as is seen in right living[4]

3, 4   Definitions from The NAS New Testament Greek Lexicon. Greek lexicon based on Thayer's and Smith's Bible Dictionary plus others; this is keyed to the large Kittel and the "Theological Dictionary of the New Testament." These files are public domain. Biblestudytools.com.

Ephesians 3:19 uses both words when Paul prays for us "to know [*ginosko*, intimate knowledge] the love of Christ which surpasses knowledge [*gnosis*, intellectual knowledge], that you may be filled up to all the fullness of God" (NASB). That word "surpasses" could also be translated as "transcends" or "goes beyond."

Gnosis is a great thing. *Gnosis* and *ginosko* are not at odds with each other. I see them as two sides of a coin. The point here is that possessing a deep intellectual understanding of Christianity, even to the point of teaching and preaching it, does not lead to life eternal. That is the result of relationship.

John 17:3 gives a super straightforward definition of eternal life: "Now this is eternal life: that they know [*ginosko*] you, the only true God, and Jesus Christ, whom you have sent."

Jesus is also using the word *ginosko* in Matthew 7:21–23 when He says, "Not everyone who says to Me, 'Lord, Lord!' will enter the kingdom of heaven, but only the one who does the will of My Father in heaven. On that day many will say to Me, 'Lord, Lord, didn't we prophesy in Your name, drive out demons in Your name, and do many miracles in Your name?' Then I will announce to them, 'I never knew [*ginosko*] you! Depart from Me, you lawbreakers!'"

Don't miss the power of this statement: it's like Jesus is saying, "I never knew you as a husband knows his wife." Although *ginosko* can refer directly to sexual intercourse, of course in this context of Christ and the bride, it is not a sexual reference. At the same time, everything that occurs in the natural world points to a spiritual reality, and this level of intimacy is no exception. Ephesians 5:31–32 says that the joining of a man to his wife as "one flesh" is a picture of Christ and the church.

This imagery brings up some significant

parallels between human marriage and spiritual oneness with Jesus. Perhaps the most obvious of these is that fruitfulness is designed to flow signed to flow out of intima-

> FRUITFULNESS IS DESIGNED TO FLOW OUT OF INTIMACY.

cy. Yet some prefer to practice a kind of spiritual *in vitro* fertilization.

In other words, they do not want to be personally intimate with Christ. They instead look to a human "spiritual father" to give them "seed" based on that person's revelation and experience with God. They amass ministries, churches, even "spiritual children"—all without spiritual intimacy. The spiritual children birthed into such a scenario are left with confusion as to who their father really is.

I know some readers may be uncomfortable with such a graphic illustration. But I think it is a vital point—a prophetic parallel between what is going on culturally in our era and what is happening spiritually.

When I think about a *ginosko* relationship with Jesus, I think of a relationship of full disclosure. The garden of Eden gives us a natural picture of this. Adam and Eve walked with their Creator naked and unashamed (Genesis 2:25).

> THERE WAS NO HIDING UNTIL THEY DOUBTED THEIR CREATOR'S HEART AND WILL.

There was no hiding until they doubted their Creator's heart and will. Lucifer planted doubt in Eve's mind that maybe the Creator was hiding something from them. Maybe He was holding out on them, even withholding something that was beneficial. That seed of doubt destroyed the innocence and closeness they shared with Creator God. Doubt turned to disobedience, which led to their separation from God.

But Jesus refused to let that separation last. He took the steps needed to open the door to the garden of intimacy once again. He reversed the curse we brought on ourselves. He did it for anyone who will let faith lead them to obedience through surrender. For all who will exchange their fear and suspicion for hope and love.

For those brave souls who crave full disclosure over hiding, intimacy with our Creator has been reinstated!

THE LONGING OF GOD

Regardless of what is going on in my life at the moment I can usually think of a song to provide the proper soundtrack. Honest confession: it's often not a Christian song. In fact, most of the time it's a love song (or even a heartbreak song) from which I draw a spiritual parallel. This book is no exception.

As I prepared to write this chapter, the tune "Alone" was running through my head all day— leading up to this point in time where I'm sitting on my living room floor with my laptop, attempting to articulate something of profound importance to me.

"Alone" was made into a hit song in 1987 by the band Heart. As my friends will attest, I typically avoid '80s music as I would influenza. Even though I was born at the dawn of that decade, I have no nostalgia about it whatsoever. I am a minimalist, and '80s culture epitomizes too much. Too much hairspray, too much synthesizer, too many color combinations, not to mention the bangs—just too much.

So when this song is coming through MY speakers, it will most likely be a version recorded twenty years later.

The song "Alone" paints the picture of a lonely soul calling someone she loves in the dead of night. But she is thwarted. She leaves a message, and instead of her phone ringing back, the minutes drone on in silence. She is losing hope that she will get a response from him at all. She is now keenly in touch with feelings that she was previously oblivious to or at least suppressed: loneliness, and the longing to be one-on-one with him.

She has been awakened to a passion in her heart for closeness but feels isolated because her feelings have not been fully expressed and therefore cannot be returned.

Independence and indifference have been overtaken by a gripping desire to be alone with the one to whom she wants to reveal her new-found love.

The spiritual parallel hit me hard. I want all that remains of my independence and indifference to be overtaken by a gripping longing to be alone with my Maker.

For your husband is your Maker—His name is Yahweh of Hosts—and the

Holy One of Israel is your Redeemer;
He is called the God of all the earth.
(Isaiah 54:5)

A parallel song is "Lonely Alone" recorded in the '90s by Reba. It talks about the quandary of being in close physical proximity to someone who is emotionally disconnected from you.

This story-song concludes by saying, "If I have to be lonely, I'd rather be lonely alone." From the moment I heard that song, it deeply resonated with me.

I would venture a guess that most of us know how it feels to love someone deeply without that love being reciprocal. Or is it just me? There are people I would give my right arm for who won't make time to go to coffee with me. But I've learned that if I succeed in convincing someone to spend time with me when they are not into it, the outcome is highly disappointing.

Isn't it the worst when you want to have a heart-to-heart talk with someone who is on their phone or looking over your head while you're together? I don't think anyone likes feeling invisible.

Maybe I tend to feel more deeply than most people. But at the very least, I think we all know how it feels to be in a crowd and still feel alone. Some of my loneliest moments in life have been in a crowd. Sitting alone in an airport on Christmas Day during a layover. Surrounded by people, lights, movement, and noise, yet the loneliness is tangible.

THERE ARE DIFFERENT TYPES OF LONELINESS AND LONGING.

There are different types of loneliness and longing. At times, I have felt this emotional alienation even while engaged in conversation. Whether it is a close relative or merely an acquaintance looking at me, I still feel invisible if I am not truly seen and known.

A lack of proximity does not create this breach. In fact, the physical presence of someone who is emotionally oblivious to me only exacerbates the frustration.

When they see what they want to see, or who they perceive me to be, instead of who I truly am, *I would rather be lonely alone*.

Conversely, when I feel accurately seen and known, my heart is content and at rest.

I am spoiled, because not only am I known by my Creator, but my life is richly blessed with friends who truly know me and with whom I get to live and minister.

They know how I will react to a situation before I have a chance to respond. They love me despite the fact that I am a bit of a zombie before I get my coffee in the morning. They know the issues I have no tolerance for, like racism and abuse. They know that although most of the time I value healthy eating, one of my comfort foods is deep-dish pizza.

I deeply love them because they truly know me, and therefore they can truly love me back.

There is no substitute for this kind of knowing and being known. It's a nice gesture when someone approaches me after hearing me speak and says, "I just love you!" but my thought is always, *How can you? You don't know me.* They don't know how frightening I look when I am sick. Or how grumpy I feel when I'm overtired. Or that I rarely dress like I have for this event, because I often work from home with no makeup, in my Captain America pajamas with my hair up in a messy bun.

I believe this human craving to be truly known is one of the ways in which we are "made in God's image" (Genesis 9:6). I think God feels the same way toward us. He wants us to know Him as intimately as He knows us. This is quite a challenge coming from a God who knows how many hairs are on our heads (Matthew 10:30)!

Do you think I'm crazy to believe that our Creator could long so deeply for our genuine attention and affection that He could pen a song like "Lonely Alone"? Do you think the longing of His heart to be near us is satisfied by our bodies sitting in church while our minds are elsewhere?

Listen to what He says in Isaiah 29:13:

> These people say they are mine. They honor me with their lips, but their hearts are far from me. And their worship of me is nothing but man-made rules. (NLT)

The King James Version words it like this:

> This people draw near me with their mouth, and with their lips do honour

me, but have removed their heart far from me, and their fear toward me is taught by the precept of men.

Our Creator longs for us with an unfathomable love. In Ephesians 3:14b–19, the apostle writes,

> I fall to my knees and pray to the Father, the Creator of everything in heaven and on earth. I pray that from his glorious, unlimited resources he will empower you with inner strength through his Spirit. Then Christ will make his home in your hearts as you trust in him. Your roots will grow down into God's love and keep you strong. And may you have the power to understand, as all God's people should, how wide, how long, how high, and how deep his love is. May you experience the love of Christ, though it is

too great to understand fully. Then you will be made complete with all the fullness of life and power that comes from God. (NLT)

What is so interesting about this Scripture is that it's saying that even though our Creator's love is incomprehensible, there is a wholeness and groundedness that comes from experiencing it in increasing measure.

> EVEN THOUGH OUR CREATOR'S LOVE IS INCOMPREHENSIBLE, THERE IS A WHOLENESS AND GROUNDEDNESS THAT COMES FROM EXPERIENCING IT IN INCREASING MEASURE.

This tells me that inside of us is a greater capacity for extravagant love and extreme worship than has been awakened. No matter where we are in this relationship, we can go higher, and wider, and longer, and deeper.

We find this longing of the Creator for an intimate relationship with His people expressed throughout the Scripture. Read Hosea: *heartbreak and longing*. Read Song of Songs: *passion and longing*.

In Jeremiah 3:19–22 the LORD says to Israel,

> I thought: How I long to make you My sons and give you a desirable land, the most beautiful inheritance of all the nations. I thought: You will call Me, my Father, and never turn away from Me. However, as a woman may betray her lover, so you have betrayed Me, house of Israel. This is the LORD's declaration . . . they have perverted their way; they have forgotten the LORD their God. Return, you faithless children. I will heal your unfaithfulness.

Again, this is an expression of heartache and longing.

In Matthew 23:37 we see Jesus crying out, "Jerusalem, Jerusalem! How often I wanted to gather your children together, as a hen gathers her chicks under her wings, yet you were not willing!" That verse has always gripped my heart. Jesus is saying, "I wanted . . . but you were not willing."

My desire is that this would not be said of me or my generation. I don't want to see us miss such an incredible invitation—to be family to Jesus! What an offer! What in this whole world could be more worth our time and attention?

Maybe what has kept you at a distance is not indifference but feelings of unworthiness. If you are struggling with feeling unwanted or too flawed to be loved by God, let me just speak to your heart: no matter how life or even your own choices have marred you, your Creator wants to restore your dignity and His unblemished artistry in you. Don't stay at a distance when the true love of your life is waiting for you to come.

> YOUR CREATOR WANTS TO RESTORE YOUR DIGNITY AND HIS UNBLEMISHED ARTISTRY IN YOU.

In the garden of Eden, the Creator came walking in the cool of the day and called out, "Adam, where are you?" I hear Him calling still today to you and me: "I see you there, but how do I get you alone?"

Are you interested in searching out this great invitation along with me?

It may mean removing obstacles—like Lucifer's age-old lie that our Creator is not trustworthy. We need to learn from the original fall in Eden to discover how not to make the same mistakes. It's way past time that we stop entertaining the slithering lies and accusations of the deceiving serpent and get him under our feet.

Today is the day to begin reclaiming the level of relationship that was meant to be yours with your Creator. It is the only thing that will satisfy His heart—and it is your inheritance as a child of God.

9
A GARDEN IN TOWN

For nearly seven years, I had the blessing of living in a beautiful lake home with a hammock on my porch. Once a day, when the light hit the lake just right, it looked like the water was covered in sparkling diamonds. Friends loved visiting for a lake retreat, and I enjoyed summers of sunbathing on the dock and jumping into the lake to cool off. It was a good season of life. My Creator truly led me, as the psalmist wrote, "by still waters to restore my soul" (Psalm 23:2–3).

Then I moved into the heart of town, where I'm living as I write this book. This is also a good season of life. The setting and soundtrack have simply changed. These days, porch time looks and sounds quite different.

Early on, as I spent time with my Creator over morning coffee at this new house, I started to look for the spiritual pictures in the scenario I was surrounded by. Around me are noisy traffic, occasional sirens, and children shouting at the nearby school. But in the midst of the noise, my little lot of land looks like the local nature preserve. So far this morning I have watched five squirrels, a groundhog, and a pregnant cat, and I've listened to the songs of several varieties of bird. I may or may not have recently spotted a mouse (and I may or may not be in denial about it).

I'm dreaming of hiring someone to take out the scrappy trees in the yard, because although

I want to think I have the agility of Tarzan, the fact that I've already fallen out of a tree while climbing up a vine says I am more like Jane. But I'll manage much of the hard work of pruning out the dead limbs, and ultimately landscape this small plot of ground into a beautiful spot. It will take effort, time, and money, but I am starting to get a vision for how inviting this wild, rough patch can be. All it will take is a bit of investment.

Living here is a very clear prophetic picture to me of the fact that I need to learn how to cultivate my inner life with my Creator in the midst of the noise—to shut out the distractions I hear and see around me. This was easy when I lived at the lake. Other than an occasional boat passing by, it was quiet and still.

This season of life has new challenges, in the natural and in the spiritual realm, and I have to grow and adapt. Instead of being disappointed in what I lost, I've taken it as an exciting challenge. I know greater revelation waits for me if I am willing to embrace the change as an opportunity to go deeper into the heart of my Creator regardless of what is happening around me.

I admit I have daydreamed about living in a convent with no distractions from prayer, studying Greek, meditating on the Scriptures, and studying church history. (No kidding, I am that much of a geek.) But then I snap back to reality—I have books to design, bills to pay, people to love, and uh-oh, I am almost out of coffee, so I definitely have to go grocery shopping today!

The good news is, I can maintain a constant dialogue with the Holy Spirit. I have an app on my phone to look up Greek definitions while I'm standing in line at the grocery store. My mind can meditate on the Scripture while I am driving across town, and once in a while, I get a slowed-down day to curl up and read the accounts of reformations and awakenings from days gone by.

For the most part, I can feed my spirit and mind while doing daily life. Other times, I simply need to stop everything and remind myself that my Creator is God and I am not. I need to take deliberate moments to be awed by how powerful He is and to let myself be as small as I actually am. Sometimes I need to stop trying to solve all the world's problems and be reminded that I am not the world changer—Jesus is.

> I NEED TO TAKE DELIBERATE MOMENTS TO BE AWED BY HOW POWERFUL HE IS AND TO LET MYSELF BE AS SMALL AS I ACTUALLY AM.

So I present myself to Him, for personal connection first and service second. If my motivation is not love for Him alone, my life focus will get off track. No other force is strong enough to keep me aligned with Him.

The day in which we live is noisy and filled with distractions. We can be so preoccupied that we don't even notice our spiritual hunger. We have to learn how to unplug, unwind, and be refilled by basking in the love our Creator has for us.

Alone in His presence is where I am filled and fueled. Sometimes that means lingering long with Him by a placid lake, and other times it means catching a few minutes on a noisy back porch.

Whatever it means for you today, take the time to be with Him. There is nothing more vitally important.

10

SACRED COMMUNITY

I have a confession to make: I avoid typical prayer meetings. It's not that I dislike prayer—it's just that to me, it often seems more like we are praying to each other than we are appealing to the courts of heaven. We don't admit it, but Protestants pray to the saints too—the ones sitting across from us in prayer meeting.

Joking aside, there are exceptions to my tendency toward avoidance. When a group of people genuinely love each other and are serious about collectively touching the heart of our Creator with heartfelt intercession and thanksgiving, I am all in. Sign me up.

At this season in my life, I am thankful to have a group of kingdom sisters to meet with once a week to worship, study, and pray. We give hugs and cheek kisses and get right into looking for what the Holy Spirit wants to do in our time together.

We worship and study. We talk through deep heart wounds, give praise reports, sometimes offer confessions and requests, and of course we pray. The Holy Spirit is always the most honored guest in the meeting.

This kind of fellowship is possible because we are worshipers. We worship throughout the week. Some of the women (I admit I am not in this class) even wake up in the middle of the night to meet with Jesus for warfare, intercession, and worship.

Being around these sisters is a breath of heavenly air.

I don't go to meetings in search of my Creator's presence. I often feel His Holy Spirit most tangibly when I am home alone. I have been overwhelmed by His presence to the point of tears while eating lunch by myself in my dining room. I don't need to leave these four walls to find Him. He is here with me and in me. And I don't meet with my faith-family out of religious duty. I don't sense more of God's approval because I attend prayer meeting.

So why go?

I go to learn from those older and wiser than me.

I go to be sharpened, as it says in Proverbs 27:17: "Iron sharpens iron, and one man sharpens another." I don't want to become dull.

I go to share. I don't want to hoard what the

Holy Spirit teaches me.

> I, ALONE, AM NOT
> THE BRIDE OF CHRIST.
> I AM A PART OF THE BRIDE.

Mostly, I go because I am a part of them. I, alone, am not the bride of Christ. I am a part of the bride. And He loves it when we are together in unity.

To me, community with kingdom family is more important than social status, location, financial security, career, image, or comfort. I've chosen my people over these things and inherited a beautiful life as a result.

I am very thankful to have an older brother and sister who have set a good example of steadfast faith for me and our younger siblings. But even if you do not have biological brothers or sisters who walk with their Creator, Jesus wasn't kidding when He said, "There is no one who has left house, brothers or sisters, mother or father, children, or fields because of Me and the gospel, who will not receive 100 times more, now at this time—houses, brothers and sisters, mothers and children" (Mark 10:29–30).

The nice thing about being part of a close-knit group of kingdom family is that it's hard to hide. When others know you well, you pretty much stay under the spotlight. Business with your Creator and each other tends to stay current. Doing life together helps us all stay on track and move forward in our walk with the Father. Like it or not, humanity has a flocking instinct, and when we are in a group it is natural to move in the same direction.

It is an interesting thing to have a personal relationship with my Creator while also being a part of something so much bigger. We experience a reliance on each other that is healthy and natural for a body. Don't get me wrong: I can't vicariously live the Christian life through your experience, and you cannot ride on my spiritual coattails. Redemption is a personal work of grace. We must obtain it individually. Yet, it is a beautiful thing when we come together to live it out and express our appreciation for it corporately.

Let me give you an example.

When I was in my early twenties, I had a friend I rarely saw, but during those precious times of connecting, one of my favorite things to do was pray with her. Well, sort of. To say "with her" is kind of a stretch. We were in the same room. But she would be "gone," in her own world with Jesus.

Sometimes she would lie on the floor, and sometimes she would pace. Other times she would go from sitting to jumping up and down. But most of the time, I wasn't paying attention to her, because I was also focused on our Jesus. (Jesus is the only Man who two women can be passionately in love with and that not be a problem!) Our love for Him was even stronger than our love for each other, and it made her my closest friend.

It's critical that we cultivate our inner life with God—and also that we come together regularly in fellowship with each other. See, mothers can come together to encourage each other, show off their babies, and let them play together, but those babies were made in private. This is an analogy for how I see the fruitful Christian life.

Being alone with our Creator is paramount. Otherwise, our "fruit" or our "works" may be illegitimate, as Jesus explained in Matthew 7:23 when He wouldn't acknowledge the good deeds that were being boasted of because "I never knew [*ginosko*] you."

Even genuine corporate worship, and a community overflowing with love for each other, are birthed in the secret place. We give out of the love we ourselves receive from the Source of our life. Then, as we bring all our hearts of love and devotion together as one, those attributes are amplified.

Again being brutally honest, I feel the same way about church services that I do about prayer meetings. If the act of gathering is coming out of obligation or mere tradition, and not heartfelt love for our Creator *and each other,* I would rather stay home.

I know some people have the philosophy that "a bad church is better than no church." Personally, I find few things more painful than passionless church services. But when the bride of Christ unites hearts to worship the Bridegroom—that is something entirely different.

Rather than showing up hoping that God's presence will come because of the anointing on the worship leaders, the best meetings are when we all come like Mary with her alabaster jar and pour out our oil of intimacy on Jesus's feet. I have been in both settings, and the difference is palpable.

Hebrews 10:25 says, "And let us not neglect our meeting together, as some people do, but encourage one another, especially now that the day of his return is drawing near" (NLT). This verse is often quoted to try to keep people from staying home from church on Sunday morning—but I believe its real meaning goes much *deeper*. This verse reminds me that my life is not supposed to be "just me and Jesus." I am not the body of Christ on my own; I am only a part of His body.

> WHEN OUR CREATOR CAME TO EARTH TO RESTORE OUR BROKEN RELATIONSHIP WITH HIM ... HE WAS HANDS-ON.

When our Creator came to earth to restore our broken relationship with Him, He took on human flesh. He walked, talked, touched, and healed. He was hands-on.

He gathered a group of followers around Him, who became His friends, and He stuck with His crew throughout His ministry. He didn't do life and ministry in isolation. He was showing us how it should be done: together, in relationship. When Jesus left this earth, He commissioned us to pick up where He left off. His redeemed children are His new body on earth.

Our personal relationship with our Creator should never be at odds with finding our place in kingdom community. These are two sides of a coin. Salvation itself is adoption into God's family. So naturally, from that moment on our spiritual life is a journey of getting to know our heavenly Father and our spiritual family.

I've have had many conversations with people who insist that there are no "good churches" in their area and therefore they have no community. My answer is: *then it's time to move.* I did. I majorly uprooted my life to be part of the kingdom community I believed would help me grow into who I was meant to become. It came at some great personal cost, but the return has been priceless.

Some people will take the argument a step further and insist, "I don't need to be in a church to be close to God. I can be just as close to God sitting on my couch at home." But my question is, *are you?* Are you as close to God as you want to be? Is He as close to you as He wants to be?

> WHERE IS YOUR HEART
> IN PROXIMITY TO
> THE HEART OF JESUS?

Whether you are at a church, or at home on your couch, where is your heart in proximity to the heart of Jesus?

My personal experience has been that when we get close to the heart of our Creator, we discover that loving Him means loving the rest of His creation.

During a very painful time in my life, I told Jesus I would serve people but I didn't think I could love and trust them anymore. He didn't correct me immediately. He just let me go and do my thing for a while . . . working for people in the trenches with no heart connection to them. But over time as He healed my heart, He showed me in no uncertain terms that my plan was not a long-term option.

I needed to be grafted back into His body, not in a universal sense, but in a *tangible,* local sense. I needed people to consistently love me

I NEEDED PEOPLE TO CONSISTENTLY LOVE ME DEEPLY AND OCCASIONALLY CHALLENGE ME HONESTLY.

deeply and occasionally challenge me honestly.

I was convicted by Scriptures like this:

> Dear friends, let us continue to love one another, for love comes from God. Anyone who loves is a child of God and knows God. But anyone who does not love does not know God, for God is love. God showed how much he loved us by sending his one and only Son into the world so that we might have eternal life through him. Dear friends, since God loved us that much, we surely ought to love each other. No one has ever seen God. But if we love each other, God lives in us, and his love is brought to full expression in us. And as we live in God, our love grows more perfect. We love each other because he loved us first. If someone says, "I love God," but hates a fellow believer,

that person is a liar; for if we don't love people we can see, how can we love God, whom we cannot see? And he has given us this command: Those who love God must also love their fellow believers. (1 John 4:7–9, 11–12, 17, 19–21, NLT)

Jesus has passionate followers scattered across the globe. Finding and building community with those in proximity to you is like a treasure hunt. It's not always easy, but it's well worth not giving up.

Some days, when relationships get hard, I have to fight the urge to let my introverted soul go nuts and just decide to be a hermit. I have to *remind myself* that I really do love community, and kingdom family is imperative for my growth and development.

But at the end of the day, I'm so glad I'm not on my own.

There was a time when I lost faith in king-dom family, but loving Jesus means also loving those He loves—and the real miracle is that they have loved me back.

We were made to walk closely with our Creator *and* with each other.

11

IN THE VOID

I will give you the treasures of the darkness and riches from secret places, so that you may know that I, Yahweh, the God of Israel call you by your name. (Isaiah 45:3)

Whenever I read this obscure passage, my mind goes back a few years to an evening worship service when Jesus came to me. He had something He wanted to show me. I didn't see Him. I only felt the evidence of His presence.

But where He took me changed my perspective forever.

Initially, I was very hesitant to put this account out into the world. People can be critical and suspicious of those who talk about visions and supernatural experiences, even though we have scriptural accounts of people like Ezekiel, Daniel, and John the Beloved having visions and being taken places way wilder than any modern accounts I've ever heard. But as I prayed about whether I should write this and release it publicly, Jesus's words from Matthew 10:27 came to mind: "What I tell you in the dark, speak in the light. What you hear in a whisper, proclaim on the housetops."

As you will see, those words are extremely apropos.

I was at the front of the church, just a few feet from the speakers where the music blared. I was thankful to be in this place as I poured my heart out to Jesus. Surrounded by people worshiping I stood, hands stretched out side to side, eyes closed, singing, "My hands are up . . . take me deeper . . ." With my eyes still closed, I felt cool air moving through the fingers of my right hand.

At first, I did not know what it was. I was trying to figure out how this sensation was isolated to just my fingers. If it had been air conditioning, for instance, I would have felt it all over me, or at least on my right arm.

Plus, the ceiling on the building was several stories high, and no air vent was in sight. As I was searching for a logical explanation, what happened next ended all natural possibilities. I began to feel bursts of air, about the size of a fist, at various places alternately up and down my outstretched arms. The temperature of the air grew warm, like breath. I finally became aware that it *was* breath.

When I realized what I was feeling, I shot a glance around me. No one was close enough for me to feel them breathing. Then I recognized that it was Jesus. I could sense Him standing right in front of me. After a few moments of His invisible form being so close that I could feel His breath on my skin, like a kiss without contact, He stepped through me. Then I felt His breath on the back of my neck.

After a few more moments, He wrapped me up in a tight embrace. Immediately, we were in a free fall into a hole that opened up directly under me.

After the plummet ended, it was as if we had plunged into the center of the earth. It was completely silent. There was literally no sound— nothing but total darkness. Nothing. My reasoning mind began to question the theology of this moment. If I was with Jesus, how could we be in pitch-black darkness? Isn't He light? But then I noticed that I felt the greatest peace that I have ever known. There was nothing "dark" about this blackness. It was simply void. I couldn't see anything, but I felt total peace. Intoxicating peace mixed with anticipation.

There was no fear anywhere in this place. We had "landed" in the same position that we left the worship service. My arms were folded across my chest, and I could still feel Jesus behind me, completely enveloping me in His embrace. It was as if we were suspended, weightless, almost without gravity, and yet we were completely still.

Then out of the total darkness, I saw a baby in a glow of light, and I heard, "This is where I formed you." The infant in front of us had dark hair, which puzzled me at first because I thought He was saying she was me. I did not ask Him about it, but I concluded that the infant was not me. We were in the present time, not in my past. I looked on with awe and said, "Show me more!"

He was silent.

I felt like He was smiling, though.

I did not want this moment or the feeling in this place to end! I wanted to stay here with Him. Forever.

As I looked at that beautiful baby in front of me, I wanted to know what Jesus was thinking when He made me.

Impulsively, I asked if I was beautiful to Him when He made me. I immediately felt embarrassed that I had asked such a shallow question. But He said, with such gentleness, "Yes."

Again, I asked Him to tell me more. But I began to feel myself moving back into the earth realm. I could feel that total peace and safety slipping away, and I would have done anything at that moment to stop time. I didn't want to go back! *Ever.*

I felt almost frantic trying to hold on and not be "sent back" to "real life." I asked one last thing, and that was, "Why did You create me?"

As I transitioned back to the worship service, I could once again hear music blaring. I could see the lights; people were still dancing around me, totally unaware that anything unusual had just happened to me. I was in the same spot, but instead of standing I was crumpled down on my knees. I don't know how long I was "gone," but I do know that the band had moved on to a different song. The song now playing was based on the Lord's Prayer and the kingdom coming to earth.

My body was still bent low, and I heard Him tell me to stand and declare His kingdom; this was one of the reasons I was here on earth. To proclaim the kingdom of God and, in some way which I still do not fully understand, bring heaven to earth. So while the music played, I stood and declared at the top of my voice, "Yours is the kingdom! Yours is the power! Yours is the glory forever and ever!"

I was grumpy for days after that. I would barely speak, and I didn't know how to talk about what had happened. I was dissatisfied with everything that would usually bring me joy.

Finally, my friend who was attending the conference with me asked me what my problem was. My problem was that I had been ruined for the ordinary. I had experienced a reality that made this one pale in comparison.

Although this experience was tangible and amazing, I wanted a theologically sound explanation for what had happened. When I expressed this to a friend, she immediately said, "Go read Psalm 139." I was floored by the details I had overlooked in this Scripture before:

Where can I go from your Spirit? Where can I flee from your presence? If I go up to the heavens, you are there; if I make my bed **in the depths**, you are there. If I rise on the wings of the dawn . . . **even there your hand will guide me, your right hand will hold me fast**. If I say, "Surely the darkness will hide me and the light become night around me," even the **darkness will not be dark to you**; the night will shine like the day, for darkness is as light to you. For **you created my inmost being; you knit me together in my mother's womb**. I praise you because I am fearfully and wonderfully made; your works are wonderful, I know that full well. My frame was not hidden from you **when I was made in the secret place, when I was woven together in the depths of the earth**. Your eyes saw my unformed body; all the days ordained for me were written in your book before one of them came to be. How precious to me are your thoughts, God! How vast is the sum of them! Were I to count them, they would outnumber the grains of sand—when I awake, I am still with you. (Psalm 139:7–18)

Once the angst of "being back" wore off, I realized the gift that I had been given. Not only had I received a confirmation of my life purpose (and come away with an incredible love of Psalm 139), but something even more important had transpired. I now realized something in the deepest part of me that before I had only known in theory: if I had nothing except the tangible presence of Jesus completely enveloping me, not only would I be content, but I would also be more at peace than I have ever been in my entire existence.

I still long to be back in that place with Him. Nothing but Jesus was more than I ever could have imagined.

> NOTHING BUT JESUS WAS MORE THAN I EVER COULD HAVE IMAGINED.

So now, getting practical, the challenge is this: how am I supposed to function in this earth realm while longing so deeply for another reality?

Before this experience, I had a harder time grasping the hype about living forever. It sounded exhausting, to be honest. But now I just want to be with Him, wherever He is. I see how life with Him is something I would never want to end.

More than ever, I want to help others awaken to this eternal reality that is more real than the temporal world we are living in.

We don't have to wait for heaven to be with Jesus. He wants His kingdom, which ultimately culminates in what we often call heaven, to permeate earth—and He wants it to happen in and through us.

Most of us have heard the King James Version of this prayer of Jesus since we were young:

> Our Father which art in heaven,
>
> Hallowed be thy name.
>
> Thy kingdom come.
>
> Thy will be done on earth,
>
> as it is in heaven.
>
> Give us this day our daily bread.
>
> And forgive us our debts,
>
> as we forgive our debtors.
>
> And lead us not into temptation,

but deliver us from evil:

For thine is the kingdom,

and the power, and the glory,

forever. Amen.

(Matthew 6:9–13)

This prayer means more to me now than it ever has before. I want to see our Creator's kingdom of light invade and push back the kingdom of darkness, which has been given so much free rein in our world. This flame of passion in me was fueled by an intimate experience with nothing but Jesus that wrecked me for the ordinary.

Jesus is better than anything I have ever experienced. I want to share this reality with the world. But it begins and ends with Him in that sacred space.

To schedule an author interview,
email: one11ministries@gmail.com

1:11 MINISTRIES
WORD. DANCE. MUSIC.

Live productions, events, and books to
inspire and empower the body of Christ.

For more information about 1:11 Ministries
visit online: **one11ministries.com**

Email us about bringing Mercy to your church,
conference, or event: **one11ministries@gmail.com**

FEARLESS

You can live free from fear.

Fear steals our lives from us. It steals our impact and cripples our joy.

In our modern world, there are a million reasons to be afraid.

But what if your default mode was courage and faith, not fear and timidity?

True freedom is possible— through the presence of Jesus and the practice of His Word.

In this book, we expose the insidious roots of fear and explore the answers found in the Bible. Learn how:

- THE FEAR OF THE LORD WILL BREAK THE POWER OF LESSER FEARS

- HOLINESS WILL CHANGE YOUR IDENTITY— AND GIVE YOU COURAGE TO STAND AGAINST THE TIDE

- THE PRESENCE OF GOD IS THE ANSWER TO THE WORLD'S TROUBLES

- YOU CAN PRACTICE THE GIFTS OF POWER, LOVE, AND A SOUND MIND

Available from Amazon and everywhere books are sold.

TIME TO ALIGN:
FREE EMAIL COURSE

Join Mercy Hope and the 1:11 team for a personal journey through 8 key areas of life in our free email-based course, "Time to Align."

This free, 11-week course is a spiritual recalibration: a chance to bring your heart, soul, mind, and strength into alignment with the nature and will of God.

To get your first lesson straight to your inbox, sign up here:
One11Ministries.com/Align